Emotional Maturity

Discover How to Control Your Emotions and Be More Mature

by Charlotte Maloney

Table of Contents

Introduction

Emotional maturity is the process of being able to respond to situations and interactions with full control over one's emotions. And let's face it: this type of self control can be difficult to achieve. There are so many factors we lack control over in our everyday lives, so we tend to act on our negative feelings. This is an easy, visceral action. It is normal to feel something and act on it, or react to it. It feels as though we are being true to ourselves.

But this uncensored, disorderly expression of emotions is the opposite of what it means to be emotionally mature. To be emotionally mature, one must think critically about one's own actions and maintain empathy. One must be able to regularly, nay constantly, maintain self-awareness. Take a bird's eye view of your own emotions to determine whether acting impulsively, from your emotions, is the best option for the situation. One must be willing to accept others as they are, because it is often interactions with others that lead to expressing ourselves without restraint.

Emotional intelligence is the art of reacting intelligently. When you react with emotional intelligence, you are confronting each situation with awareness and deciphering the best response while being true to your character.

Mastering one's emotions can be more complicated than checking off a simple task list. It is a process that requires constant practice and revision. In the following pages we will discuss the fundamentals to emotional maturity that, if internalized, can result in a different worldview which promotes maturity in your actions and reactions.

Chapter 1: Ways to Balance the Ego

Not reduce, not banish. Balance! Ego is an essential part of ourselves. It allows us to focus attention on ourselves in order to pursue our ambitions and present ourselves favorably. It sets each one of us apart from the others. But in such a self-centered age, where we are constantly assessing how we present ourselves to others and interpreting others by how they have chosen to present themselves, ego plays an oversized role in society. We have more exposure to each other's shells than what lies beneath, meaning we are inevitably motivated to focus on these shells.

To separate the ego from the self, it is important to bring self-awareness into our lives. The simplest way to begin: **sit still for ten minutes each day, close your eyes, straighten your spine, and watch your thoughts go by**. You will learn to disassociate yourself from the thoughts that float through your mind.

Think about it this way. **The ego is fragile and innocent, like the case of a glass lantern.** If there is no candle lit within, the glass case of the lantern is guarding nothing substantial. By not lighting a candle within, and cultivating the self, all that is left is the glass case or the ego. The fragility of the ego becomes us and overwhelms us. It serves no purpose and instead gallivants as a reason for existence in itself. But the ego is a shield and it requires something deeper below. It is the lantern which guards the flame from being blown out, and it must be balanced with deeper sustenance so that we may find deeper purpose. This deeper sense of purpose, something that comes from within, is an indispensable necessity in sustaining emotional maturity.

That being said, it is not all about you and your agency. Much of the world functions by forces we cannot explain. So **do not take anything too seriously.** Honestly speaking, we could do without most of what we humans produce on this planet. There is less need than you think for all the theories, all the news, all the junk we produce. There are brilliant accomplishments of mankind, yes. But if you are agonizing over something, worrying about perfecting it, or trying to get it to change, remember this: in the grand scheme of things, the world will continue, we will all die, and it does not make a big difference how it works out. Appreciating the size and depth of the universe around us, and recognizing how minuscule we are on our "pale blue dot," lessens the size of the ego and the need for it to be so large and pampered.

Another thing that helps us move away from ourselves and connect is to **love easily**. When we connect to others, we realize the beauty of giving and getting love. It is a fundamental that we all search for, and when you become comfortable with treating all living beings with respect, love automatically follows. Love does not have to be romantic, or platonic, or for that matter it does not have to fit into any particular definition. Do not limit the kindness, graciousness, and respect with which you treat others. On that same note, **do not try to control what others think of you. It is not your job.** The ego is governed by feeding our self-importance in relation to the universe and others. But your self-worth is not defined by others.

Work hard. Working hard is an excellent form of devotion. If we find work that we can attach meaning to (and yes, we and solely we are responsible for making meaning in the world, and finding meaning in the work we do), concentrating on doing this work well is the most excellent form of building character and balancing the ego. As put by the brilliant Patti Smith, "Build a good name. Keep your name clean. Don't make compromises; don't worry about making a bunch of money or being successful. Be concerned about doing good work. Make the right choices and protect your work. And if you can build a good name, eventually that name will be its own currency. Life is like a roller coaster ride, it is never going to be perfect. It is going to have perfect moments and rough spots, but it's all worth it."

Chapter 2: How to Act Instead of React

When you surrender to the ego, it is difficult to find purpose and we become guided by those around us. We become forces of reaction, rather than self-guided action that comes from a sense of self within. Therefore, it is important to develop the self. To do this, it is important to live in the present. Do not hold grudges or blame the past. There is nothing you can do about it. Instead, focus on the opportunities available to you at every moment. Do not react in spite when you feel wronged, or slighted, or treated unfairly. This *reaction* is the central tendency in emotional immaturity. By responding to the stimuli around you, you are governed by them. If you *act* instead, by proactively treating others with respect, maintaining a focus on adding value to your life, and choosing your battles, you will open doors that you could not have foreseen. Essentially, reacting is harmful and immature because it comes from an assumption that whatever is happening in front of your eyes represents the full set of possibilities as to what can happen. But by *acting* you are expressing to the world and the universe the true nature of your character, and you will attract the people and opportunities that are in line with your true nature. To do this naturally, you need to know yourself and respect yourself.

Know what you are seeking. This is slightly different from knowing what you want, because it involves an element of foresight. For example, if you are aware of what you want, you can recognize if you are hungry and want a donut. This is a more basic, animalistic form of self-awareness. But if you know what you are seeking, you are thinking about your own future and preparing to meet it with your best self. A practical way to do this is **each day to do one thing that will benefit you five years from now.** Whether that be exercise, eating healthy, sorting out your financials, or working on a skill; think in terms of *value added.* By working on yourself, and learning to think in a forward-looking mindset (while focusing on your actions in the present, without dwelling or obsessing about the future), you can equip yourself to confront any situation with a clear mind and act rather than react. You are building yourself, which grounds your emotional maturity in a real sense of confidence and self-assuredness.

Choose your battles wisely. Moment to moment, you are a sum of emotions and thoughts. So it is important, if you find that something makes you emotional, to step back and reflect on whether you want to fight this battle – whether or not you want to pour emotions into it. This is related to the earlier exercise of knowing what you are seeking. Those who are emotionally mature know when to fight, and when not to. If you are getting caught up in a situation, and find yourself exasperated or frustrated, take a step back. Take a few seconds to breathe deeply and assess exactly what you are upset about. Then think, is this worth the frustration? If it is not important in the grand scheme of things (however you choose to frame it), recognize that you need not devote the emotional energy towards the situation. But maybe it is an important issue. Maybe it is an important project at work that you do not want your colleague to botch. Maybe it is a struggle to make decisions with an aging parent. If it is important, recognize that your emotions may be hijacking your ability to act effectively. They are making you *react*, rather than *act*. Emotions are an important tool in acting true to yourself—they are the visceral, intuitive counterpart to your right brain's tendency to intellectualize problems. They show you whether or not you *care* about something. So do not ignore your emotions. Instead, recognize them, step back to make sure they are not overpowering your ability to act, and determine how you can channel them to act in a productive manner. If you are able to do this, you will become a master of emotional maturity.

Make 'genuine respect' your mantra for interacting with others. All those seeking emotional maturity are not going to act in the same way. There are infinite personalities and thus infinite ways of being true to yourself. This changes not only across people but over time—you become wiser the more of life you have the privilege of seeing, and it modifies the way you interact with others. But no matter what form your interactions take (whether you are sarcastic, or jovial, or you seldom talk), it should be guided by genuine respect for others. This does not mean you have to agree with them, or always be in a splendid mood. Rather it is a recognition that just as you are formed by your nature and a lifetime of experiences, others are informed by those factors that have shaped their worldview. Respect is an understanding that you are no better than someone and always willing to learn from them. By using respect as a guide for your interaction with others, you will think twice about yelling at someone when you are angry, put them down, or hold grudges.

Chapter 3: What It Means to Accept without Judgement

Everyone has a lot going on, including you. By accepting the simple fact that everyone is carrying some burden, and there are always factors in any situation that you cannot account for, it becomes easier to react rationally to a situation. So **practice acceptance of others.** Do not judge them, especially not for things they played no part in, like physical appearance. Be willing to admit when you are wrong.

Practice acceptance of yourself. Remember the quote from Albert Einstein that goes, "Everybody is a genius. But if you judge a fish by its ability to climb a tree, it will live its whole life believing that it is stupid." This doesn't necessarily mean you are brilliant and are failing due to an idiotic, opaque system. Rather, the key is that in this quote, you are both the "you" and the "fish." **Do not conceptualize yourself** — accept yourself, your body, your abilities, and cultivate your strengths rather than berating yourself for your weaknesses. By creating an identity for yourself, you are getting in the way of *just being.* When reverting to this calmer, stronger state of mind, you have the ability to take a bird's eye view of your emotions and where they stem from. Negative emotions like jealousy and self-doubt often arise when there is an incongruity between what you are and who you think you ought to be. If you have no expectations, you are better able to face reality for what it is, and act wisely without letting your emotions control you. Another key to accepting yourself is to know that **you are not worth what you were born with**—be humble about that which you did not earn: your beauty, your family's wealth, the status that has given you access to security.

Finally, it is important to **accept the situation**. Again, you are better able to face reality for what it is if you have no expectations, meaning you can act wisely without letting your emotions control you.

While it is important to live in the present, you have to spend some time with your past and the future in order to function effectively in the present. Emotional maturity involves being able to take responsibility for your own actions, and at the most basic level, there are certain needs we need to cover, like it or not, to function and prosper in the world. Some basic planning, like the fundamental of personal finance and an awareness of how to maintain a healthy diet, puts you in a place to maintain a strong base on which to build yourself.

Emotional maturity is hard to maintain without maturity in other aspects of your life. Thus, if you are not in control of the situation, it is easy to become overwhelmed by life.

Respect the way the world works. This is fundamental to operating within it in an empowering way. For example, one of the most ubiquitous (and to many, repugnant) realities of the world we live in is… money. Money is a necessity. Respect this. It is not necessary to obsess over it and make it the center of your activities, but it is important to learn to manage it so it doesn't manage you. Avoid debt because it is one of the scourges of human civilization. Make sure you save, so you have the flexibility to live life as you choose—to act rather than react. As Albert Einstein said, "Compound interest is the eighth wonder of the world. He who understands it, earns it. He who doesn't, pays it."

Chapter 4: The Importance of Adopting Flexibility

"The only true wisdom is in knowing you know nothing." - Socrates

We are molded by our past experiences. We are molded by the world around us. But if we think everything around us in the world is set in stone, we feel powerless and cease to be able to do anything to change it. One of the most powerful things a person can realize is aptly summed up by Steve Jobs: "When you grow up you tend to get told that the world is the way it is and you're job is just to live your life inside the world. Try not to bash into the walls too much. Try to have a nice family life, have fun, save a little money. That's a very limited life. Life can be much broader once you discover one simple fact: Everything around you that you call life was made up by people that were no smarter than you. And you can change it, you can influence it… Once you learn that, you'll never be the same again." By being open-minded and flexible, you open up the possibility of changing the world around you. As a result, you become more proactive rather than responsive to your emotions.

Flexibility allows you to adjust yourself to each situation. You bend as necessary, rather than being inflexible and butting heads with the situation. This allows you to take advantage of the situation and turn it into something valuable, even a learning experience, rather than give a negative response guided by your emotions. **Life is not about the situations you are confronted with, it is about how you confront a particular situation.** There are several different ways to practice this simple but powerful concept.

Everyone can teach you something. **There are no friends and no enemies, only teachers.** Take a moment to consider how your interactions with others would change if you approached them with fewer preconceived notions. For instance, you could approach each situation thinking, "there is something here for me to learn from." This is an extremely valuable mindset if you want to emotionally mature. It brings a lens of critical reflection to all your interactions, combined with empathy for others. It helps you respect others without a second thought, and helps you rise above a difficult situation or interaction with maturity and aplomb.

Judge your own thought patterns, not someone else's. What about the situation is causing me to act this way? What beliefs are guiding my response? These are the questions that come to the mind of an emotionally mature person when they are in a tricky situation. Rather than lashing out, they are able to take a step back and assess their reactions silently. By assessing your thought patterns regularly, you are in effect creating a mental log. You will be able to see, over time, which of your beliefs and what about the situation is making you act a certain way, and this attunes you to your unique profile of emotional responses. Over time, you are not only able to control the effect of your emotions on your responses, but also appreciate that you can change your thought patterns. In the same way people quit smoking or other addictive behaviors, you can recognize patterns of thought that lead you to destructive emotions, and figure out a way to either avoid the situations or rationalize your emotional response in a different direction.

Experience. Travel the path less taken. By seeing more of the world, we begin to see both how differently people live their lives as well as the underlying rhythms of life. We realize that many of these differences run only so deep. **Learn something new every day.** This does not mean you have to cram it into your head, remembering everything you encounter, but sit with the idea for a few minutes and consider your own thoughts on it. Your thoughts, not what you are supposed to think. By exposing yourself to new things, you broaden your understanding of what exists out there and how people think, and this in turn makes you aware of the sheer number of possibilities. The power of education is to open up the world to you, and allow you to realize that there are equally an infinite number of ways you might open up to the world. By recognizing that there are so many possibilities, you have the option of confronting situations in more productive, positive ways. **Go towards your fears.** This is an excellent mantra if you want to continue to challenge yourself. If something scares you, it can also be interpreted as something you have left to confront and conquer.

Chapter 5: Portraying Confidence and Assertiveness

Assertive behavior, the practice of **balancing your needs with the needs of others**, is the communication style of those who are emotionally mature. Assertion is a habit in opposition to passivity, which prioritizes the needs of others, and aggression, which prioritizes your needs.

Know thyself. Bring mindfulness to all your actions and consider whether this is exactly how you want to react.

Choose your words wisely. Before you speak, think about what you are going to say and consider what it is contributing to the conversation. These days, there is a culture of talking. Those that speak loud and formidably clear get the attention, even if they are not saying something of substance. But there is great power in choosing your words more carefully. Developing this habit manifests in your thought process—by speaking less you listen more. You reflect more. Ultimately, you absorb more and are better able to discern whether there is something substantial to contribute. As you speak less, you will find that there is often not that much to say. Speaking with discretion promotes integrity of your word and is a reflection of emotional maturity.

Learn to say no, straightforward and diplomatically. These days, we are always busy. It is a sign of power and success to be busy. But you should not get trapped in situations that make you more emotionally aggressive just because you do not feel comfortable refusing. Learning to say no is about knowing yourself and what you want, and knowing how to avoid situations that are emotionally volatile or unproductive for you. Learning to say no helps you focus on your strengths, and cultivate confidence and a sense of self that is a necessary base for emotional maturity.

Do not do anything that you have to apologize for. This is a great rule of thumb to follow, because integrity is important to having peace of mind. To please others, we often make promises big and small that we cannot keep. Assertive behavior recognizes the need to acknowledge others' needs, but it also demands that you acknowledge the following: to maintain a healthy self and a vital, mature personality, you need to know your limits. By double-checking your actions to make sure you are not hurting others, you are cultivating a self that is capable of handling its emotions in a healthy way. Keep in mind that people also often say "sorry" too much, and that should be separately acknowledged if it is an issue. And if your actions do not hurt anyone, remember the maxim: it is better to ask for forgiveness than permission!

Conclusion

Emotional maturity is, by definition, the ability to control your emotions in response to situations. But the stoic who barely reacts is not necessarily mature. Emotional maturity involves the ability to be self-aware of one's emotions and be able to filter them before acting on them. Whether you are relatively unemotional or life feels like a constant, erratic roller-coaster, emotional maturity involves being able to respond wisely in each moment while staying true to yourself.

Adopting such a process is based on balancing or keeping the ego in check, and accepting your circumstances. With practice, you will develop an automatic filter in which you ask yourself, regularly and with little effort, "how is this making me feel, and how do I really want to respond?" By detaching your emotions from your reactions, you are empowering yourself. By separating your emotions and your actions, you gain the ability to look at things from a bird's eye view and put things into perspective. You easily understand what is important, and just as importantly, what is not. You have the ability to accept how you feel in this instant, but also discern how to act in a way that benefits you now and in the future. Moreover, this self-awareness comes with a bonus realization that others are just the same. Everyone is a mishmash of experiences and feelings and thoughts, and this empathy turns on a light bulb under which you can understand them better. Then, you can treat them better. This will start a feedback loop of positive responses in which your maturity influences your actions, which get you further and increase your confidence in order to make you all the wiser and more mature.

Emotional maturity is essential in the process of growing as a person. While it takes time and effort, it is a wonderful investment to make. There is peace when you know how to self-reflect easily, and small shifts in interacting with the world around you can make all the difference. So go ahead. Using these tips, start today and supercharge your life.

Finally, I'd like to thank you for purchasing this book! If you found it helpful, I'd greatly appreciate it if you'd take a moment to leave a review on Amazon. Thank you!

Made in the USA
Middletown, DE
09 July 2022